THE CHINESE LADY

BY LLOYD SUH

THE CHINESE LADY
Copyright © 2019, Lloyd Suh
All Rights Reserved

ISBN 978-0-8222-3990-1
www.dramatists.com
www.concordtheatricals.com

THE CHINESE LADY is fully protected under the copyright laws of the United States of America, and of all countries covered by the International Copyright Union (including the Dominion of Canada and the rest of the British Commonwealth), and of all countries covered by the Pan-American Copyright Convention, the Universal Copyright Convention, the Berne Convention, and of all countries with which the United States has reciprocal copyright relations. No part of this publication may be reproduced in any form by any means (electronic, mechanical, photocopying, recording, or otherwise), or stored in any retrieval system in any way (electronic or mechanical) without written permission of the publisher.

The English language stock and amateur stage performance rights in the United States, its territories, possessions and Canada for THE CHINESE LAD are controlled exclusively by Dramatists Play Service. No professional or nonprofessional performance of the Play may be given without obtaining in advance the written permission of Dramatists Play Service and paying the requisite fee.

This work is published by Dramatists Play Service, an imprint of Concord Theatricals Corp.

All other rights, including without limitation motion picture, recitation, lecturing, public reading, radio broadcasting, television, video or sound recording, and the rights of translation into foreign languages are strictly reserved.

For all inquiries regarding motion picture, television, online/digital and other media rights, please contact Dramatists Play Service, an imprint of Concord Theatricals Corp.

MUSIC AND THIRD-PARTY MATERIALS USE NOTE

Licensees are solely responsible for obtaining formal written permission from copyright owners to use copyrighted music and/or other copyrighted third-party materials (e.g. artworks, logos) in the performance of this play and are strongly cautioned to do so. If no such permission is obtained by the licensee, then the licensee must use only original music and materials that the licensee owns and controls. Licensees are solely responsible and liable for clearances of all third-party copyrighted materials, including without limitation music, and shall indemnify the copyright owners of the play(s) and their licensing agent, Dramatists Play Service, an imprint of Concord Theatricals Corp., against any costs, expenses, losses and liabilities arising from the use of such copyrighted third-party materials by licensees. For music, please contact the appropriate music licensing authority in your territory for the rights to any incidental music.

IMPORTANT BILLING AND CREDIT REQUIREMENTS

If you have obtained performance rights to this title, please refer to your licensing agreement for important billing and credit requirements.

The co-world premiere of THE CHINESE LADY was presented at Barrington Stage Company (Julianne Boyd, Artistic Director; Branden Huldeen, Artistic Producer), Pittsfield, Massachusetts, July 2018. It was directed by Ralph B. Peña, the scenic and costume designs were by Junghyun Georgia Lee, the lighting design was by Oliver Wason, the sound design and music composition were by Fabian Obispo, and the production stage manager was Geoff Boronda. The cast was as follows:

AFONG MOY .... Shannon Tyo
ATUNG .... Daniel K. Isaac

THE CHINESE LADY was commissioned and co-world premiere presented by Ma-Yi Theater Company (Ralph B. Peña, Artistic Director) in New York City.

THE CHINESE LADY was developed with support of the Roe Green Award at Cleveland Play House.

Additional thanks to Claudia Alick, Christine Bruno, Nancy E. Davis, Loretta Greco, Sonia Fernandez, Andrea Hiebler, Laura Kepley, Peter Kim, Kimber Lee, Rachel Lerner-Ley, Teresa Avia Lim, Gregg Mozgala, A. Rey Pamatmat, Haleh Roshan Stilwell, and Krista Williams, all of whom contributed in essential ways to the development of this play.

CHARACTERS

AFONG MOY, female, from fourteen years old to advanced age.

ATUNG, male, older than Afong Moy.

SETTING

The United States, beginning in 1834.

NOTES

The characters should be played by Asian or Asian American performers. They should speak in their natural and organic speaking voices, with no affected dialect or accent (the lone exception is in Scene 3, when Atung performs multiple voices). Otherwise, the characters should simply talk the way the actors talk.

While acknowledging that there is a distinction between the historical practice of foot binding and a contemporary model of Disability culture, the relationship of audiences to Afong Moy's feet was certainly influenced by historical perceptions of disabled bodies. In an ideal circumstance, the role of Afong Moy would be played by a performer with a similar physicality to the historical Afong Moy. While further acknowledging that feet like Afong Moy's no longer exist, I encourage producers to seek out and consider performers with physical or mobility disabilities.

The text of the play acknowledges that the performers' bodies are not the bodies of their historical counterparts. The production should as well. Regardless of whether or not the performers have physical disabilities, at no point should they pretend to a type of mobility that they do not possess. In some cases, of course, this may mean that certain physical actions described in the play may not occur literally. As with their speaking voices, the characters should simply move the way the actors move.

THE CHINESE LADY

Scene 1

Lights up on Afong Moy, fourteen years old, in her Room. The Room is a box placed in the center of the larger stage. Outside the box, the stage is unadorned. Inside the box, it is ornate, decorated with various types of Chinoiserie. Watercolor paintings, vases, curtains, silks, furniture, etc. She wears a traditional Chinese gown and jade or lacquered jewelry in her hair.
Afong begins the scene seated. Atung sits on a plain-looking chair, downstage of the Room.

AFONG. Hello. My name is Afong Moy.

It is the year 1834.

I am fourteen years old, and newly arrived in America.

I was born in Guangzhou Province in 1820. I am one of seven children, the youngest. My family has sold me for two years of service to Misters Nathaniel and Frederick Carnes, traders of Far East Oriental Imports to New York. I will be on display here at Peale's Museum, for your education and entertainment, at a price of twenty-five cents adults, ten cents children.

Thank you for coming to see me.

She bows.

ATUNG. I am Atung. I am

AFONG. Atung is irrelevant.

ATUNG. I am irrelevant, that's what I was going to say, I was going to say I am irrelevant.

AFONG. Atung has been in service to Misters Nathaniel and

Frederick Carnes as a manservant and translator of Chinese to English and back again. He is now assigned to me.

ATUNG. You do not need to know who I am or where I come from, or how it came to be that I speak both languages with such practical and occasionally poetic fluency. Only that I will assist Afong Moy, The Chinese Lady, during all exhibition hours.

AFONG. We will not be needing Atung's translation services for the time being, for I am not speaking. It would of course seem that I am speaking, as my mouth is moving and my thoughts are becoming articulated through sound, but this is not in fact what is happening. What is happening is a performance. For my entire life is a performance. These words that you hear are not my own. These clothes that I wear are not my own. This body that I occupy is not my own. This Room in which I am seated is intended to be representative of China, just as I am intended to be representative of The Chinese Lady: the first woman from the Orient ever to set foot in America, and yet this Room is unlike any room in China, and I am unlike any lady to ever live.

And yet here we are. You and I.

ATUNG. And Atung.

AFONG. And Atung, who is irrelevant. Seated in this Room in this museum, in this exhibition hall advertising The Chinese Lady.

I shall assume that you have paid your twenty-five cents, ten cents for children, because you are curious about China. Curious about what a Chinese lady might look like or act like. I have not been in this country long enough to know the ways in which I might differ from other ladies you have encountered, or what your particular curiosities might be. But I have been told to highlight certain features that I possess, as they may seem exotic and foreign and unusual to you.

I understand it is my duty to show you things that are exotic, and foreign, and unusual.

At the start of every hour, I sit down and stay seated. I watch the customers enter the exhibition hall. I do not move. Some customers stand quietly and expectantly, while some come directly towards the Room and examine its contents. They look at the furniture. The vases. The silks and the paintings. They talk to each other. Oh look at that. I've never seen such a thing. It reminds me of. I wonder if. What do you think it feels like? And they look at me. They look at my eyes. They look at my hands. At my clothes. At my hair. At my face.

They say things to each other. Do you think she… I wonder if she… And my goodness look at her feet.

Allow me to explain my feet.

In many parts of China, it is considered a sign of elevated social status and cultural refinement for women and young girls to have tiny feet.

When I was four years old, my feet were placed into a hot mixture of herbs and animal blood to soften the skin and muscles. My toenails were clipped to their smallest possible size. Both feet were then deeply massaged and oiled before the toes were broken by hand and bound flat against the soles, into triangles. My arches were bent, then bound in silk ribbons. These ribbons were wound in a figure-eight motion, multiple times, pulling the ball of the foot and heel together, and pressing the toes underneath the sole.

This continued for about a year, every few weeks, the bones broken, then set, then broken again.

And for this part of the exhibition, I walk. In one revolution around the Room, to illustrate and demonstrate the form and function of my feet.

> *She walks.*

ATUNG. Typically, during this part of the show I am the one who describes the process of foot binding to the audience. But I do not need to do that now.

AFONG. Because I already did.

ATUNG. Because she already did.

> *Afong Moy finishes her long revolution around the Room and sits.*

And now I will bring her food.

> *Atung exits.*

AFONG. Next, I will eat, and you will watch me. Atung will bring to me plates of steamed shrimp and Chinese vegetables, along with a pot of tea which I will pour and drink in a ritualistic way so as to demonstrate its importance in my culture.

Atung enters with a tray of food and tea.

ATUNG. Shrimp and Chinese vegetables. Pot of tea.

AFONG. I will eat these foods with chopsticks.

She displays the chopsticks with a flourish.
She takes a bite.

Since arriving in America I have been living in a small room in the home of Mrs. Augusta Obear, wife of the ship's captain who brought me here. It is a lovely home with details quite peculiar and novel to my experience. The foods I have been eating there take some getting used to. There is much bread. There is much corn. There is much potatoes. I am unaccustomed to such foods. As is my digestive system.

Perhaps she burps.

The room in Mrs. Obear's house is quite different than this Room, though the Obears have added a few artifacts from China to the decor, presumably to make me feel more at home. These accents are comforting despite their inauthenticity, but I am even more appreciative and fascinated by the differences. I have been sleeping on a bed that is elevated some three feet above the floor. I hope I do not fall off of it!

Also, everyone wears their shoes inside the house! A curious phenomenon.

I am ambivalent about the fork. I have seen it in use and I understand its functionality; it seems a useful tool for the stabbing of food, but ultimately I feel it lacks grace. Chopsticks are elegant and poetic. Forks are violent and easy.

She has finished her food.

I am finished, Atung.

ATUNG. Very well.

Atung takes the food, leaves the tea, and exits.

AFONG. Now I will pour the tea.
>   *She does.*

In China, tea is of the utmost importance. There are many kinds of teas, for various uses; it is as much for pleasure and entertainment as it is for health and medicine.

The story goes that over four thousand years ago, the Chinese emperor Shennong would boil his water before he drank it so that he could be sure it was not contaminated. One day, while traveling outdoors, a leaf from a wild bush fell into the water and steeped itself in the cup. He did not notice this leaf, and to his surprise he drank the very first cup of Chinese tea.

I like this story because it tells us that history is an accident.

The accident of tea has changed the course of history, and without it I would perhaps not be here with you today.

Let me put it this way.

It is human nature to be curious. Curiosity is evolution. We migrate, from the trees, through the jungle, across oceans and rivers, we are constantly searching. This is what sent the Carnes brothers to China. This is what brings me here. We want to see. It is the same impulse that brought you here, to this Room, to me. You want to look at me. You want to understand more about the world. You want to understand more. More. More.

I will discuss the history of tea in greater detail at a later time.

For now, thank you for attending this presentation of The Chinese Lady.

I am very pleased to be here in this great country. I am very pleased to represent my homeland, my family, my culture, and my history to you in hopes that this may lead to greater understanding and goodwill between China and America, and between all the peoples of the world!

>   *Atung enters and draws a curtain across the Room.*

Scene 2

Atung opens the curtain across the Room. Afong Moy sits, as before.

AFONG. Hello. My name is Afong Moy.

I came to America in 1834, when I was fourteen years old.

It is the year 1836, and I am sixteen years old.

The price of admission to Peale's Museum has increased, and I am grateful that you have deemed me worthy of such an honorable price as fifty cents adults, twenty-five cents children. I hope that I can entertain and educate you well enough to justify such a luxurious amount.

The agreement between the Carnes brothers and my father was that I would spend two years here, in exchange for a fee.

Those two years have now expired, yet here I am.

Why am I still here?

This is a complicated question.

I have only recently come to understand the magnitude of my presence here. So far in the history of America, there have been a very small number of Chinese men who have migrated in pursuit of work in merchant or mining trades. Some have been granted less strenuous labor. Like Atung.

ATUNG. I do alright.

AFONG. But there has never been anyone like me.
I am the first Chinese woman you have ever seen.

I am the first Chinese from nobility, the first educated Chinese, the first with bound feet, the first the first the first.

And so you see, this gives me a great responsibility.

This exhibition has become the most popular attraction in the history of Peale's Museum, and I am delighted to share with you the news that starting next week, we will begin a forty-week tour of the

Eastern United States, in some fifteen different cities, where I will be on display for people all across this great land.

I will be in Boston. Philadelphia. Baltimore. Such a nice name. Baltimore. Washington, D.C., named for your first emperor, George Washington. I delight in this. I will go to Providence, Cincinnati, Pittsburgh. How I long to see Pittsburgh.

How strange it is that I will now learn far more about America than I ever knew about my homeland.

Perhaps when I return, I will travel China as well. In much this same way. Perhaps I can travel to various cities there, and impart to the villagers all the lessons I have learned in America.

But no, perhaps what I should do… ah yes! I just had a wonderful idea. Perhaps I should hire a fourteen-year-old white American girl to come with me to China, and display her in a room with a raised bed, shoes on her feet in the home, eating with a fork! Perhaps I can tour her throughout the country and let the Chinese look at her and study her, put her on display for the education and edification of the Chinese curiosity!

And then I could be like Atung. Ha! Couldn't I?

ATUNG. Or I could.

AFONG. Oh. Yes, I suppose that's true, Atung, you could serve the same function to the white girl.

ATUNG. I would like to return, someday, to China.

AFONG. How long have you been in America, Atung?

ATUNG. A long time.

AFONG. This is unspecific, Atung, how long?

ATUNG. I suppose since I was…oh, fourteen?

AFONG. And how old are you now?

ATUNG. I am as old as the wind.

AFONG. What?

ATUNG. I am as old as the hills.

AFONG. Atung no you're not.

ATUNG. I am as old as the rain.

AFONG. The rain is eternal.

ATUNG. Exactly.

AFONG. Atung don't talk nonsense. Aren't you excited to travel the country? To see Philadelphia?

ATUNG. Sure.

AFONG. To see Baltimore?

ATUNG. Baltimore, yes.

AFONG. To see Pittsburgh?

ATUNG. No, not Pittsburgh.

AFONG. Why not Pittsburgh?

ATUNG. I have been there before.

AFONG. Nonsense again! When were you in Pittsburgh?

ATUNG. I was there…a long time ago.

AFONG. Again with your non-specificity. Honestly, Atung, I must learn to accelerate my English studies so that I won't need you anymore.

ATUNG. You will always need me.

AFONG. We'll see about that.

ATUNG. You will always need me.

Silence.

AFONG. Anyway, yes, I am pleased to report I am learning English and I am doing quite well.

ATUNG. She's not doing well.

AFONG. I am a remarkable student.

ATUNG. She is hopeless.

AFONG. Soon I will be as fluent as I am in this performance.

ATUNG. No.

AFONG. Right now I can only speak in simple terms, and I fear this makes people think I am stupid. When a white person asks me a complex question, such as "Are you excited to tour the country?," I can say only "Yes" or "Oh yes sir very much," and while this might convey some enthusiasm, it cannot convey the poetry of it. If I had the words in English I would say that I cherish the opportunity like a flower cherishes sunlight, that the thought of seeing the whole of America roots in me like a jewel that has lodged inside my eyes and colors every part of my vision.

ATUNG. When she says things like this, I translate them as: "She says yes, she is excited."

AFONG. And so these white people, they think I am simple. I must not allow that. I must express my voice. This is my obligation to America. This is my obligation to the world.

ATUNG. Afong, it is time for you to walk.

AFONG. Oh! Dear yes, my goodness, how irresponsible of me. Thinking ahead to the future when I have tasks in the now.

> *She walks.*

I have noticed that my feet are a source of constant fascination. Most Americans consider it barbaric. Of course, in China there are many who feel the same way, but it is tradition, and so there is hesitancy to alter it. Personally, I don't consider it barbaric. I like my feet.

I have noticed there are traditions in the American identity that are similarly entrenched, despite some controversy about them among the populace. Such as corsets. Or the Transatlantic Slave Trade.

Perhaps this is the way of tradition. We set systems in place so that we can provide a structure. So that we can feel secure. And then, at some point, as we evolve, these systems become unnecessary. But before we can move on to a new set of traditions, we must live in a slow dismantling of the old ways. It may take time. But it is useful work.

> *She completes her revolution around the Room.*

ATUNG. And now, I will bring her food.

> *Atung exits.*

AFONG. Every evening for two and a half years, I have eaten the same dinner with slight variations. A bowl of rice and a plate of shrimp or chicken or fish, and a pot of tea.

At lunchtime, however, I eat American food. Oh it is good. I get to eat beef. And mashed potatoes. And corn. And bread. When I tour the countryside, I wonder what new and exotic foods I might have the opportunity to try.

Atung brings the food and tea.

ATUNG. Remember to watch your portion control. They pay to see a delicate girl.

Afong eats.

AFONG. I wonder if they use forks in Pittsburgh. Perhaps they use something else entirely. I wonder what other instruments might exist for the consumption of food around the world. I hope there are so many that one could not possibly try them all in a single lifetime. I hope that each city in America is as different as Guangzhou is to New York. I hope that once we travel the Eastern United States I have an opportunity to travel the West too. I have heard much of St. Louis. Of Utah and Montana, and oh man oh man San Francisco California. Has there ever been a name so beautiful as San Francisco California?

I hope that I can see it all, and beyond. See what types of foods they eat and what color their people are. What sort of rooms they live in.

Perhaps she burps.

Forgive me.

I should clarify. Because while I very much romanticize the differences between people and cultures, I am even more appreciative and fascinated by the similarities.

In order to illustrate what I mean, let us further discuss the history of tea.

Atung takes the tray of food, now finished, and exits. He leaves the tea, which Afong pours.

Tea is Chinese. It is ancient and traditional and ours. In London, the British existed for hundreds of years without it. And yet when they encountered our Chinese tea in the year 1615, it quickly became so important to them that they started wars over it. They shifted the rituals of their day to include a teatime that has now become a deeply entrenched English cultural tradition as integral to their identity as William Shakespeare or the river Thames.

Is this not comforting? It is, right? That one culture can be so moved by another that it simply cannot resist the urge to appropriate it for themselves?

Atung enters.

ATUNG. Hrmpf.

AFONG. What?

ATUNG. What?

AFONG. What?

ATUNG. What?

AFONG. Did you say something?

ATUNG. No.

AFONG. Yes you did, you made a noise.

ATUNG. Oh. That. A noise, yes, I did.

AFONG. What does such a noise represent?

ATUNG. It's just… well, I think it may be a little more complicated than you're making it sound.

AFONG. Atung, you cannot possibly object to such a beautiful example of cultural sharing, for is this not our very purpose in America?

ATUNG. There is a difference, Afong Moy. Between sharing, and taking.

AFONG. Why Atung, are you expressing a personal opinion about something?

ATUNG. Never mind.

AFONG. I've never heard you speak this way.

ATUNG. What way.

AFONG. Like there is something in this world that you care about.

ATUNG. There isn't.

AFONG. Oh come now, Atung. Don't you care about the hopeful exchange of ideas and practices around the globe?

ATUNG. Just doing my job.

AFONG. Don't you care about representing your people and your homeland?

ATUNG. I'm only here to translate.

AFONG. Don't you care about me?

ATUNG. Please just drink your tea.

> *She does.*

AFONG. Would you like some?

ATUNG. What?

AFONG. Yeah. It's sooooooo good.

ATUNG. No thank you.

AFONG. Are you sure?

> *She slurps.*

ATUNG. Yes, Afong Moy. I require nothing.

> *She finishes her tea.*

AFONG. All gone.

ATUNG. Very well.

> *Atung draws the curtain across the Room.*

Scene 3

> *Atung opens the curtain across the Room. Afong Moy sits, as before.*

AFONG. Hello. My name is Afong Moy.

I came to America in 1834, when I was fourteen years old.

It is the year 1837, and I am seventeen years old.

So much has happened and I can't wait to tell you all about it. I will save the biggest and most exciting news for last, so please be patient.

You probably cannot even tell, but this Room has been dismantled and carried by carriage all across the United States, reassembled in museums and fairgrounds in your most renowned cities. We have been to Boston. We have been to Buffalo. We have not been to Pittsburgh, but we have been to Baltimore, and it was as lovely as it sounds.

In Philadelphia I saw the Liberty Bell! They say it is the bell that rang upon the signing of the Declaration of Independence in 1776, when you overthrew the dynasty of George III. Atung has informed me that this is not a true story, and that the bell was created *after* your independence day, but I support the telling of the story as it was told to me, for it is better and more beautiful than the truth.

ATUNG. If you say so.

AFONG. I do. I do say so. For what kind of a story would it be if the bell lacked such relevance? Never mind what kind of a story, what kind of a *bell* would it be without the story? It would be insignificant, and eventually forgotten and discarded altogether. Atung, let the story live!

ATUNG. I disapprove of this.

AFONG. No one cares.

ATUNG. I know.

AFONG. Also, did you know that the bell is cracked?

ATUNG. I do know that.

AFONG. I wasn't talking to you, I was talking to them.

ATUNG. Okay.

AFONG. The crack in the bell appeared after the very first time it was rung. I think this is such a beautiful detail, isn't it? A beautiful poem, for it tells us that liberty is fragile. The crack is growing, as well. Even though the bell no longer rings, the crack continues to grow. Simply through the passage of time. This is another poem. It tells us that liberty has a cost. And an expiration.

ATUNG. Or it just means that it was badly made.

AFONG. Atung why are you so cross? Is it not a beautiful day?

ATUNG. How would I know? I haven't been outside at all, but stuck in here with you.

AFONG. And I've been stuck in here with you, yet still I feel so extraordinarily blessed. For it's now time to share the most exciting news about our trip.

ATUNG. Alright.

AFONG. Guess where we are?

ATUNG. Washington, D.C.

AFONG. NOT YOU ATUNG, I WAS TALKING TO THEM!

ATUNG. Sorry.

AFONG. You've spoiled the surprise! I wanted to be the one to say it, and I also wanted to hear what guesses they might have before telling them. It was going to be fun, but now it's not fun. Oh Atung you ruined my delivery.

ATUNG. So sorry.

AFONG. And yet you will not ruin my mood! For yes, we are in Washington, D.C., your national capital! And please do not be jealous, but here is the best part: I have just returned from a private meeting with your emperor, Andrew Jackson. It was just the two of us!

ATUNG. And me.

AFONG. Oh yes, the two of us and Atung. Speaking of Atung, Atung is

ATUNG. I'm irrelevant.

AFONG. I wasn't going to say you're irrelevant.

ATUNG. Oh.

AFONG. I was going to say you could be of great use at the moment. For I have had an idea!

ATUNG. Uh-oh.

AFONG. Why uh-oh?

ATUNG. I do not like your ideas.

AFONG. I have extraordinary and wonderful ideas!

ATUNG. You have dangerous and incomprehensible ideas.

AFONG. No I never.

ATUNG. It was your idea to go swimming in the Susquehanna River.

AFONG. That was amazing!

ATUNG. It resulted in pneumonia.

AFONG. And memories.

ATUNG. And two canceled performances.

AFONG. Well this idea is splendid, and shall delight us both. For in order to illustrate the extraordinary conversation I had with Emperor Jackson, a simple description will not suffice; Atung as you were there, let us…recreate the dialogue together!

ATUNG. Wait what?

AFONG. We shall play-act the conversation. I will speak what I spoke, and you will speak what he spoke.

ATUNG. What about what I spoke?

AFONG. But you merely spoke what he spoke and I spoke.

ATUNG. Oh. Right.

Silence.

AFONG. Wait a moment. Atung. You did, right? You did not mistranslate any of our words, did you?

ATUNG. Of course not.

AFONG. Atung.

ATUNG. It's just that there are sometimes words or phrases which do not directly translate from Guangzhou Cantonese to American English, so the act of translation is more like…interpretation than direct recreation.

AFONG. What?

ATUNG. Yes. Even as we play-act our roles, this is but an interpretation. For this is not then. I can present to you a memory of someone, but it will only be a performance. The words you hear will not be theirs. The clothes I wear will not be theirs. The body that I occupy will not be theirs. Like cracks in a bell or a story of when it first rang, we can only simulate the past, not in pursuit of the literal truth but some other less-tangible truth about ourselves and the nature of truth itself. Mmm.

AFONG. Oh so now you like the story of the bell.

ATUNG. I didn't say I like it, I'm just saying it's similar to the act of translation; it's a fact whether I like it or not.

AFONG. Very well then, you can play-act your own self and the emperor.

ATUNG. President.

AFONG. What?

ATUNG. Forget it.

AFONG. Come up here with me.

ATUNG. Wait what?

AFONG. I said come up here with me.

ATUNG. Up there?

AFONG. Yes.

ATUNG. But. That… oh no. I don't think I should, that is not my place.

AFONG. Please, Atung. I need you.

> *Silence.*

ATUNG. Do I have to?

AFONG. I need you.

> *Silence.*

ATUNG. Very well.

> *Atung sits. He is remarkably comfortable in this play-acting— he performs both himself and Jackson with conviction.*

AFONG. It is my humblest and most treasured privilege to meet you, most esteemed Emperor Jackson Your Highness.

ATUNG. It is pleasure to meet President sir.

(As Jackson.) Marvelous!

Good!

AFONG. It has been my great honor to be a guest in your most powerful and benevolent nation, and it is my hope that my presence here can lead to greater understanding between the peoples of China and America.

ATUNG. Thank you much for let me be inside America. I hope Americans will like Chinese.

(As Jackson.) I do like Chinese yes, in fact I've often found Oriental people to be quite winsomely exotic.

I admire the Chinese people very much for their many fine qualities.

AFONG. And I admire the American people for their boundless curiosity and fierce individuality.

ATUNG. American people also good I think.

AFONG. I have had the great privilege of seeing so much of America, and have been performing to sizable crowds the very same performance I have shown to you today.

ATUNG. I am so happy. Many Americans see me.

AFONG. While I am extremely pleased to be admired in this way, I cannot help but wonder if there is more I can do to bring our cultures closer together.

ATUNG. Maybe I can do better.

AFONG. I feel my fame has provided me a tremendous opportunity to share more about who we are; not simply on the surface levels of clothing and adornments, but a deeper, more lasting intimacy.

ATUNG. I am famous. I want you to know who I am.

AFONG. Through such proximity and visibility, we might be able to share the very best parts of Chinese culture and American culture with one another, in pursuit of greater empathy and commonality.

ATUNG. Become close… um, yes. We become close. We become more the same.

AFONG. I wonder if Your Highness may have ideas on how to utilize this platform in more ambitious ways?

ATUNG. Does President Jackson think performance is good or can maybe be better?

(As Jackson.) Oh I think the performance is marvelous.

He thinks the performance is good.

(As Jackson.) I wouldn't change a thing.

He would not change a thing.

(As Jackson.) I would like to touch your feet.

He would like to touch your feet.

> *Silence.*

AFONG. What?

ATUNG. It is not so typical for such a thing.

(As Jackson.) I am not a typical person.

He says he is…strange man.

> *Afong offers a foot.*

Atung as Jackson is delicate.

(As Jackson.) It is at once disgusting and mesmerizing.

You are beautiful in your ugliness.

He releases her foot.

(As Jackson.) I would like to visit China one day.

I wish to go to China.

AFONG. I am so pleased to hear you say this.

ATUNG. Happy for you go to China.

(As Jackson.) Alas I probably won't have the chance, not for some time. The British are on the verge of war with China. Opium War, they call it. Dirty business, and no it's not our war but we do have interests. I have no love of the British obviously, but there's money in opium, money in tea. The trade routes are lucrative and so it behooves us, you understand.

Um. Please to say again, more slow?

(As Jackson.) Ah, never mind, it's over your heads of course.

So sorry I no can understand.

AFONG. Atung, what is he saying?

ATUNG. *(As Jackson.)* This was a marvelous diversion. I've always adored carnivals and freak shows. As a boy I would delight in them, and it's been a long time since I've recaptured the memory. I must take my leave now, and turn my attention to more important matters.

Silence, as Jackson leaves.

AFONG. Atung, what did he say?

Silence.

ATUNG. He said… He said that. You, Afong Moy, are a special and most outstanding person, and your work in this country is an important step in the fruitful exchange of cultures and in the promotion of world peace.

AFONG. He said that?!

ATUNG. He did.

AFONG. It did not seem that he was saying such things.

ATUNG. Well he did. He did say them. I only… you see, I only hesitated because he spoke with such beautiful prose, a type of elevated lyricism that I could not so promptly translate. I needed a moment to best consider how to articulate his most excellent message of hope and gratitude for all that you are, Afong Moy.

AFONG. Oh wow.

Atung stands, and then takes his place in his regular chair downstage of the Room.

Yes it was a most marvelous meeting.

Silence.

Atung, are we not behind schedule?

ATUNG. Oh. Yes, of course.

AFONG. What's wrong with you today, Atung?

ATUNG. Nothing. It is time for you to walk.

AFONG. Yes! It is time for me to walk.

She stands. Begins to walk.

While I walk, let us continue our discussion on the history of tea.

In our last episode, we discussed the British appropriation of tea. British Imperial rule in the Mughal Empire allowed for the

She stops.

Atung?

ATUNG. Yes?

AFONG. Is there something you are not telling me?

ATUNG. No.

Silence.

AFONG. Okay.

She starts to walk again.

Where was I. Oh yes. Britain conquered what is now India, giving them access to fields and fields and fields of opium. The British eventually weaponized this opium, distributing it throughout China, which ravaged the countryside. This led to the first of the Opium Wars, which led to the Treaty of Nanking. At least economically, the British Empire took over China as well.

She is finished walking, but does not sit.

Atung there is something you are not telling me and I would like to know why.

ATUNG. It is none of your concern.

AFONG. Why is it none of my concern?

ATUNG. Knowing why it is none of your concern is also none of your concern.

AFONG. Is it not appropriate for me to decide what is my concern and what is not?

Atung stands.

ATUNG. Time to eat.

Atung exits. Afong sits.

AFONG. The reason Britain *wanted* to conquer China was, of course, trade routes. And the most important reason to control trade routes, of course, is the price of tea.

Of course, I do not know any of this. At least not right now, in 1837, when the Opium Wars are beginning, when I am only seventeen years old and so shielded from news of the world. I do not know that I do not know this, either. All I know is that you are looking at me, that I am presenting this image, that I have so much hope and so little reality, that the China of my mind is more and more distant every day, that the hope I hope is more and more hopeless, and with each passing hour I am less and less Chinese. Less and less Chinese, but more and more old, and therefore closer and closer to the inevitable day when you will stop looking at me altogether.

Atung brings a plate and some tea, places them before her.

Atung what is this?

ATUNG. Pork.

Atung sits. Afong picks at the pork but does not eat.

AFONG. In Cincinnati, we went to a zoo. They had many animals on display at this zoo.

I did not think very much about what the animals were thinking. If they had dreams or ambitions, or what they hoped to achieve in their lives behind glass. I admired them for the way they moved, their hair, their eyes.

If I am in a cage, what sort of animal am I?

Times I feel I am a swan or a peacock, with adornments to be admired.
Times I feel I am an ox, or a donkey, or some other beast of burden.
Times I feel I am a sheep.
Times I feel I am a tiger.

But I am none of these things, am I?

I am a human being.

She pushes the food away.

What are we doing here, Atung?

ATUNG. I don't know what you mean.

AFONG. Is it good? What we are doing? Does it matter?

ATUNG. I do not think about that.

AFONG. What do they see when they see me?

ATUNG. You cannot think about that.

AFONG. What if it is not good, Atung?

ATUNG. You have had a long and remarkable day, Afong Moy, and you should rest.

AFONG. Because I am thinking that perhaps…perhaps it is not good.

ATUNG. Please, Afong Moy.

AFONG. What if we simply do not belong here?

ATUNG. Whether we belong here or not…we are here. Whether it is good or not, Afong Moy…you. You are good. And you are tired. You must not worry yourself with things you cannot control. It is time to rest.

AFONG. NO.

ATUNG. Afong Moy.

AFONG. Atung, I

ATUNG. Please. They are watching.

Perhaps he whispers this. Perhaps he takes hold of her head,

by the chin, as if to show her the eyes of the audience.
And with that, she is silent. Perhaps she forces a smile.
He then moves to comfort her. Simple, and gentle. If she wears a headdress, perhaps he removes it for her. If her hair is tied, perhaps he loosens it.
This can take time.
She closes her eyes and rests.
Atung tiptoes towards the plate of food.
He eats. Voraciously. Heaps and heaps of food into his mouth at once.
He closes the curtain.
Lights shift a little—not much, but a little:
We are now in Atung's dream.
He stands and speaks with his mouth full.

Sometimes when I dream, I dream of China. I dream of my childhood, of sky and streams of memory, of earth that bore me and mother and father that look like me. Sometimes when I dream, I dream of ocean, and the ship that carried me to all of these new worlds.

But most of the time, when I dream, I dream of the Room.

I dream that it is *my* Room. My dress. And when the people come to look, everyone looks at *me*.

In the dream, Afong Moy is my translator.
I know it is a dream because she cannot speak for me.
No one can speak for me. In a dream or otherwise.
I speak for myself, and my voice is beautiful.

It is so beautiful that when I discover that the Carnes brothers are charging now, all over the country, seventy-five cents adults and fifty cents children, I demand that we are paid as well. I demand that Afong Moy is paid, for her translation services, but I demand that I am paid more.

In this dream, my demands are met.

Also in the dream, Afong Moy is my lover.

I know it is a dream because I have no physical desire for Afong Moy. But I also know the dream is real because I see how men look at her.

I see how women look at her too, and I see the difference. When I see the way that men look at Afong Moy, I am filled with a desire to protect her. From the dangerous eyes of men, and the thoughts that arise from a gaze of that kind.

As if she can be protected from a gaze! Her life depends on that gaze.

My dream ends with the physical act of love, between me and Afong Moy.

I will tell you a secret. I like to look at the white women. The white women with their white dresses and flowery hats, their parasols and lace. When I look at them in real life, I imagine tearing off those dresses and tossing their hats in the sea, I dream of breaking their parasols into fractions and ripping their lace from their bodies with such wild abandon it causes these women to moan in delight.

I also like to look at the white men. The white men with their ridiculous mustaches and too-tall top hats, their booming voices and splotchy skin. When I look at them I dream of biting their flesh to watch as it reddens, I dream of burying my face in the jungle of their woven hair, I dream of overpowering their maddening power with a power they've never imagined, making them submit to my charms until the volume of their voices subside in soft, supple whispers of breath, like a caress.

I know what these daydreams mean.

I have an appetite for what I cannot have.
And because I cannot have anything—
In this life, you see…I cannot have anything.
So it is natural that what I want. Is always that which is *most* forbidden.

What is most forbidden to me is not the white women. It is not the white men.

The physical act of love that occurs between me and Afong Moy… *That* is what is most forbidden. For it comes from a different impulse and a different emotion. It comes from the desire to possess. I know I can never possess a spirit like the spirit of Afong Moy. She is like a wisp, a memory, an idea, a poem. A poem about the sadness one feels after a brief fall of rain, so slight it leaves only a hint of dampness on the earth, and soon the roaming sun will evaporate completely any evidence that such a beautiful rain ever existed.

This is not something one can possess.
One can only try to enjoy it while it lasts.

In order to illustrate this point, you will not see us again for many years.

This has been my dream. Or at least, the part of my dream I am willing to tell you.

Lights.

Scene 4

Atung opens the curtain. Afong Moy sits, as before.
Perhaps the contents of the Room are sparser. Perhaps her costume is altered somewhat, in an attempt to increase the costume's appeal to men.

AFONG. Hello. My name is Afong Moy.

I came to America in 1834, when I was fourteen years old.

It is the year 1849, and I am twenty-nine years old.
Silence.
Perhaps she crosses her legs.
Before I start describing my various daily ills and the general tedium of repetitious life inside a box, allow me to fill you in on what has happened in the twelve years or so since we last spoke. Since Washington, D.C., and my triumphant tour of the United States, and my most memorable meeting with President Andrew Jackson.

First of all, yes I now know the difference between a president and an emperor.

Which is to say, my English is better than it was. You see, I am speaking English now. So what you are hearing me say is perhaps closer to what I truly sound like.

Unfortunately, however, I am starting to lose my understanding of Cantonese. I have little occasion to use the language, except with Atung. And Atung doesn't speak very much these days anymore.

Atung shrugs.

Also, I am back in New York. Or I should say, *we* are back in New York. The three of us: Me, Atung, and of course, The Room.

We are no longer employed by the Carnes brothers, who have retired from the trade of Far East Oriental Imports. Peale's Museum has been sold to our new employer, Mr. P.T. Barnum, a theatrical impresario and purveyor of exotic entertainments for the viewing pleasure of all ages. There is no longer a separate fee for viewing me in my Room, for we are but one part of a larger attraction now, and the cost of general admission to P.T. Barnum's American Museum grants each attendee access to our exhibition.

Crowds have been light, in other words.

Part of this is due to the fact that Chinese people are becoming more common in America. The Opium Wars have led to widespread hardship and instability in the Qing dynasty, and the promise of gold has brought waves of Chinese men to California. Eager to work for lower wages than their white American counterparts.

We'll see how that turns out.

She stands.

For the sake of changing tastes, it has become necessary to change certain aspects of my regular performance. But one part that has not changed is this: the part where I walk.

She begins to walk.

Speaking of walking, speaking of gold, and speaking of mass migration, here's something I learned about Andrew Jackson.

You might already know this, but when Europeans first arrived in America in 1492, there were lots of people who were already here. For the sake of clarity, let's call them Americans, and let's call people like Andrew Jackson oh let's say…European Americans.

Since 1492, European Americans colonized these lands, constructed a liberty bell, and rang that bell for their freedom. The Americans, meanwhile, were slowly forced to leave their native lands, and fight for their survival.

Here's where the gold comes in. Because the European Americans discovered that the mountains of Georgia had gold in them. Andrew Jackson said hey let's take their land so that we can better access the gold.

So Andrew Jackson decreed that all Americans east of the Mississippi River had to resettle in the West.

How did they get there?

They walked.

> *She sits.*

Usually, at this point in the performance, as you might remember, I would eat. We cut that.

Food is too expensive and Mr. Barnum insists I manage my weight.

So I just demonstrate the use of chopsticks by grasping at the air.

> *She takes a pair of chopsticks out of her hair and uses them to grasp at the air.*

Yes.

> *She puts the chopsticks back in her hair.*

I have no further insights on the subject of tea.

> *She looks around to make sure no one can see, before removing a bottle of whiskey and a glass tumbler she has concealed.*

Nowadays it's all about gold.

> *She pours herself a drink.*

Which brings me to one other thing I should mention before we jump ahead in time a little bit once more.

I've decided to retire from the entertainment business.

> *She knocks back her drink.*

Yep. See, 1849's gonna change the whole world and me right there with it. They're calling it the California Gold Rush, so I'm pulling up stakes and heading West.

> *She removes a cigarette and a match.*

Here's the secret though, see: I'm not going in search of gold. I'm going in search of more Chinese in America. I'm curious what Chinese people look like, and talk like. What the Chinese do. What they eat. How they walk. What they think about when they think about the future.

She lights the cigarette and takes a long, slow drag.

Don't tell anyone, okay? It's probably best if I just sneak out, less trouble that way. I'll see you when I get there.

Until then, thank you for coming to P.T. Barnum's American Museum.

Atung draws the curtain across the Room.

Scene 5

Atung opens the curtain across the Room. Afong Moy sits, as before.

AFONG. Hello. My name is Afong Moy.

I came to America in 1834, when I was fourteen years old.

It is the year 1864, and I am forty-four years old.

Perhaps you are surprised to see me still here.

Perhaps you had the delightful expectation that for this scene, once Atung pulled the curtain back, I would be in San Francisco, California, on a mountain high up in the Sierras, feeling the wide wild western wind in my hair, great autumn sunset behind me, and the expansive liberty of America at my feet?

No, you knew that wouldn't happen, didn't you? You knew it all along. Silly me, silly Afong Moy, for hoping it might happen.

Yeah, I'm still here.

But not for long.

To which you say: Ah there she goes again! She still thinks she can escape!

But no, I'm not talking about escape. I'm talking about being replaced. Betrayed. Discarded.

This morning I have learned that Mr. P.T. Barnum has made arrangements for the importation of a young woman by the name of Pwan Ye Koo from Peking. She is fourteen years old, her feet have been bound half an inch smaller than mine, she plays the erhu and performs improbable Chinese acrobatics, sings like a trained chorus of nightingales, and arrives in New York Harbor later this afternoon.

I am to make immediate arrangements for my departure from P.T. Barnum's American Museum.

Silence.

ATUNG. Afong Moy. It has been the honor of my life to work beside you these thirty years. I have little to show for my life. I have no money, I have no friends, I have no family, I have an aging body that will not see many days beyond this one. I have spent my life in aid to you, and it was a privilege to do so. I have watched you from the time you were fourteen years old, a beautiful ray of too-warm sunshine cutting across my hardened cheek; since that time you have experienced great disappointment in the face of your most earnest good hope. And yet you have endured. You will endure. I know this because I know you, Afong Moy. It is possible I know nothing else about this world, except that it would be a much better world if it were more like you.

Silence.

AFONG. Oh Atung. What shall we do now?

ATUNG. What do you mean?

AFONG. Where can we go?

ATUNG. Oh. Perhaps I was unclear.

AFONG. What?

ATUNG. I am staying.

Silence.

AFONG. Oh.

ATUNG. I am paid nothing. I am already here. There is no sense for P.T. Barnum to hire another to translate for Pwan Ye Koo.

AFONG. Oh.

ATUNG. It makes no difference how old I grow, how irrelevant. I am not the one they are looking at.

AFONG. Oh.

> *Silence.*

ATUNG. I

AFONG. Please leave me.

ATUNG. Afong M—

AFONG. Please.

ATUNG. I wish I

AFONG. LEAVE ME.

> *Atung hesitates, but then*
> *He bows a deep, sincere, and honorific bow*
> *Before slowly exiting.*
> *Silence.*
> *She is alone.*

I would like to share with you
I would like
some further details on the subject of
updates since last we spoke
on the subject of gold.

Gold, yes, but also
the subject of
the subject of Liberty.

Beginning last year, in 1863, work on the Transcontinental Railroad began. It is one of the most ambitious projects ever undertaken in the history of American ingenuity, and it will join East and West together.

Excuse me, I meant to say East and West *America* together, not East and West, ha.

This railroad is being constructed primarily by Chinese laborers. Many of these Chinese arrived on the Western shores in pursuit of gold. They arrived with such earnest hope, but none would find their fortune. There is only so much gold in America. It does not matter if our hope is boundless. Fortune is finite.

In the absence of fortune, to the rails they go.

Oh yeah I should mention, at this point, it is still only men.

I wonder what they would have thought of my show.

I should also mention
I have not heard
in over thirty years I have not heard
my father, you see
I sent a letter
1836 1837
when I was
1839
1841
fourteen years old
youngest of seven children
I can't remember
I can't remember their faces
I can't remember my mother
I have not heard from
for you see, The Carnes Brothers
I gave them a letter
to send
in 1836
a letter to send in 1837
and of course they never sent it
1838
why would they
1839
so many years

There are many jobs required to complete a project so vast as the Transcontinental Railroad. The Chinese were ideal for the most dangerous duties, such as clearing the terrain, leveling trees, or blasting through ancient rock and mountain formations with pick-axe and dynamite.

They needed a level field to lay down their tracks.

Building tunnels.

With gunpowder, yes, but with newer industry as well,
Nitroglycerin, mixed on-site,
Creating holes in the mountains for trains to pass.
Sometimes the mountains fought back.

But they bent the earth to their will.

Apologies.
Not their will.
Someone else's design, of course.
Someone else's map.
Someone else's vision.
But they executed that vision,
even as that vision executed…
the vision was executed
executed

The vision of course
Was Manifest Destiny
For you see
All you see
It is yours
The vision was about
more more more

I should also mention however
Simultaneous to this
As you know
There is Civil War
There is fracture
Some land you claim, but
Some land breaks away
And thus you battle
To understand the proper shape of yourself

And perhaps this is always the way.
You grow bigger
And yet you grow smaller.

Forgive me I remember something now.
I remember a girl

in Canton Province
Where was I
at a picnic I think
by the river
I think I was twelve
perhaps thirteen
I dropped my handkerchief
on accident I think
but who remembers
and she picked it up
and she looked at me
and she smiled

I wonder what she's doing now

Why am I talking about this?

What am I talking about?

I don't suppose there's a carriage?
I don't suppose I could have

Never mind

Atung?

Atung are you there?

No

In the Gettysburg Address, delivered last year by President Abraham Lincoln, he says this nation was conceived in Liberty.
The world will little note, nor long remember.
It is for the living, rather, to be dedicated here to the unfinished work.
The great task remaining before us.

I will take my leave of P.T. Barnum
I will take my leave of the Room

And you may say
But you have no skills
And you may say
But your feet
And you may say

But you have nothing
But you have no one
But you've never
and you grow old
you have lost
you are done
you are irrelevant
Afong Moy
But I will walk
to Philadelphia
where I will ring the Liberty Bell
I will walk
to Gettysburg
to Pittsburgh
where I will forge steel
I will walk
to and from Cincinnati
I will build my own carriage
I will build my own train
and from St. Louis Union Station
I will ride the Transcontinental Railroad to
San Francisco, California
and from there
maybe further
maybe China
maybe the edge of the world,
but I'll decide.

You may say
such a thing
it has never happened

And I say
I will be the first.

> *She exits the Room.*
> *She closes the curtain from the outside.*
> *She exits the stage.*

Scene 6

The curtain drawn. Afong Moy opens it herself, from behind. Atung is not there, but his chair might remain.

AFONG. Hello. My name is Afong Moy.

I came to America in 1834, when I was fourteen years old.

It is the year 1882, and I am sixty-two years old.

As you can see, I am still here.

But where is here? This is not an exhibition. This is a different space entirely, though you will please indulge me as I allow the details of where I am to remain a mystery for the time being.

In this year, 1882, Congress passes the Chinese Exclusion Act, banning Chinese migration to the United States for ten years. Those Chinese already here are forced to find refuge in new spaces, their own improvised spaces, separate spaces, safe spaces.

Like this one.

This Room was built with a hope that it might serve as a platform for understanding, for learning, for sharing.

Just as I, Afong Moy, was built with hope for understanding, for learning, for sharing.

But just as the Room did not fulfill its purpose, I offer to you, my friends, my deepest and most sincere apology. For I too did not fulfill mine.

In the year 1871, a mob of five hundred Californians descend upon the residents of Los Angeles' Chinatown. Fifty-two Chinese Americans are injured, while twenty are tortured, lynched, and displayed along the town's borders in exhibition.

Perhaps if I had done things differently.

It is the year 1885, and I am sixty-five years old. One of these safe spaces, in Sweetwater County, Wyoming, is burned to the ground by a mob of one hundred fifty white men, resulting in the mutilation, decapitation, and castration of fifty Chinese-American miners, many of whom are burned alive or left to die along the river as they fled.

It is the year 1887, and I am sixty-seven years old. The Snake River massacre in Hells Canyon, Oregon, results in the death and torture of thirty-four Chinese Americans, stripped of their gold, their bodies dumped in the river; many will not be discovered for years.

Perhaps if I had been more worthy of the task. If I had shown you more of myself. If I had walked differently. Eaten differently, provided more clarity on the metaphysical metaphor of tea, perhaps…

It is the year 1892, and I am seventy-two years old. The Chinese Exclusion Act is renewed for another ten years.

If only I could have shown you how we are so alike in many beautiful ways. And how we are so different in beautiful ways as well.

It is the year 1902, and I am eighty-two years old. The Chinese Exclusion Act is made permanent.

I am so so sorry.

We are pushed further and further away, and so we make our own space. Separate space.

Like this one.

Let me tell you about this space.

It is the year 20__ and I am _____ years old.*

Thank you for coming to see me.

I have been waiting for you for so long.

Waiting. Preparing. For this chance to try again. I hope I am worthy of the opportunity.

In anticipation of your visit, you see, I have rented this room, searched for and purchased identical versions of each artifact that was contained in the original Room, and have renovated this space to represent the Room's features.

It was the best I could do. It is but a replica, a performance. This is

---

* The year and age here should directly correspond to the timing of the performance.

not my voice, for it was never recorded; these are not my clothes, for they were not kept; this is not my body, for it no longer exists.

And yet, I hope I have been able to convey the…relevance.

I know it is human nature to forget. To think about the future more than the past. I thank you for indulging me in listening to my past; it is all that is left of me.

I have shared it with you in hopes that you might see what it means for the present, and how it might shape the future. I have shared it in the hope that you might recognize some part of it as your own.

But mostly I share it because I don't want you to forget me.

This is the part of the show where I walk.

Afong stands and begins to walk.

I walk but I am not going anywhere. I walk in a circle.

I stop when I arrive at the place I began.

She completes her revolution around the room.

The place I began was a place of endless possibility and earnest good hope. It was a place of aspiration and empathy, where we could all look upon something we've never seen before and recognize that the world is so much more vast and varied than we could ever have imagined. But if we take the time to really look at each other. To really look at each other. Then we might see, through all that vastness and variance, something true and real and wonderful.

It is a beautiful thing to look at something long enough to really understand it.

But it is so much more beautiful to be looked at long enough to be understood.

She sits.

At the start of every hour, I sit down and stay seated. I watch the customers enter the exhibition hall. I do not move.

They talk to each other. Oh look at that. I've never seen such a thing. It reminds me of. I wonder if. What do you think it feels like? And they look at me.

So let's do that.

Let's look at each other.

I'm looking at you.

Are you looking at me?

> *Perhaps the lights begin to fade.*
> *Perhaps the frame of the Room is like a picture frame.*
> *Perhaps the lights continue to fade, until she is barely seen.*

Can you see me?

End of Play

PROPERTY LIST
(Use this space to create props lists for your production)

SOUND EFFECTS
(Use this space to create sound effects lists for your production)

Dear reader,

Thank you for supporting playwrights by purchasing this acting edition! You may not know that Dramatists Play Service was founded, in 1936, by the Dramatists Guild and a number of prominent play agents to protect the rights and interests of playwrights. To this day, we are still a small company committed to our partnership with the Guild, and by proxy all playwrights, established and aspiring, working in the English language.

Because of our status as a small, independent publisher, we respectfully reiterate that this text may not be distributed or copied in any way, or uploaded to any file-sharing sites, including ones you might think are private. Photocopying or electronically distributing books means both DPS and the playwright are not paid for the work, and that ultimately hurts playwrights everywhere, as our profits are shared with the Guild.

We also hope you want to perform this play! Plays are wonderful to read, but even better when seen. If you are interested in performing or producing the play, please be aware that performance rights must be obtained through Dramatists Play Service. This is true for *any* public performance, even if no one is getting paid or admission is not being charged. Again, playwrights often make their sole living from performance royalties, so performing plays without paying the royalty is ultimately a loss for a real writer.

This acting edition is the **only approved text for performance**. There may be other editions of the play available for sale from other publishers, but DPS has worked closely with the playwright to ensure this published text reflects their desired text of all future productions. If you have purchased a revised edition (sometimes referred to as other types of editions, like "Broadway Edition," or "[Year] Edition"), that is the only edition you may use for performance, unless explicitly stated in writing by Dramatists Play Service.

Finally, this script cannot be changed without written permission from Dramatists Play Service. If a production intends to change the script in any way—including casting against the writer's intentions for characters, removing or changing "bad" words, or making other cuts however small—without permission, they are breaking the law. And, perhaps more importantly, changing an artist's work. Please don't do that!

We are thrilled that this play has made it into your hands. We hope you love it as much as we do, and thank you for helping us keep the American theater alive and vital.

Note on Songs/Recordings, Images, or Other Production Design Elements

Be advised that Dramatists Play Service, Inc., neither holds the rights to nor grants permission to use any songs, recordings, images, or other design elements mentioned in the play. It is the responsibility of the producing theater/organization to obtain permission of the copyright owner(s) for any such use. Additional royalty fees may apply for the right to use copyrighted materials.

For any songs/recordings, images, or other design elements mentioned in the play, works in the public domain may be substituted. It is the producing theater/organization's responsibility to ensure the substituted work is indeed in the public domain. Dramatists Play Service, Inc., cannot advise as to whether or not a song/arrangement/recording, image, or other design element is in the public domain.

www.ingramcontent.com/pod-product-compliance
Lightning Source LLC
LaVergne TN
LVHW051922060526
838201LV00060B/4126